Harry Hosier
Circuit Rider

Warren Thomas Smith
Foreword by Ralph E. Blanks

Abingdon Press
Nashville, Tennessee

HARRY HOSIER: Circuit Rider

Copyright 1981 by the Upper Room. Copyright assigned 1994 to Barbara Smith. Abingdon Press edition 1994.

All rights reserved.

No part of this work may be reproduced or transmitted in any form by any means, electronic or mechanical, including photocopying and recording, or by any information storage or retrieval system, except as may be expressly permitted by the 1976 Copyright Act or in writing from the publisher. Requests for permission should by addressed to Abingdon Press, 201 Eighth Avenue South, P.O. Box 801, Nashville, TN 37202

94 95 96 97 98 99 00 01 02 03 – 10 9 8 7 6 5 4 3 2 1

This book is printed on acid-free recycled paper.

ISBN 0-687-00801-8

Some of the material in this book appeared in another form by Dr. Smith in "Harry Hosier: Black Preacher Extraordinary," in *The Journal of the Interdenominational Theological Center*, Vol. VII, number 2 (Spring 1980), and is used by permission.

The scripture quotations used throughout this book unless otherwise noted are from the King James Version of the Bible.

The scripture quotations designated RSV are from the Revised Standard Version of the Bible, copyrighted 1946, 1952, and 1971 by the Division of Christian Education, National Council of the Churches of Christ in the United States of America, and are used by permission.

The drawing on the cover and on page 2 is owned by Zoar United Methodist Church, Philadelphia, Pennsylvania, and is used by permission of the Reverend Ralph E. Blanks.

The illustration on page 32 is from *An Album of Methodist History* by Elmer T. Clark. Copyright renewal 1980 by Mary Alva Clark. Used by permission of Abingdon Press.

HARRY HOSIER
Circuit Rider

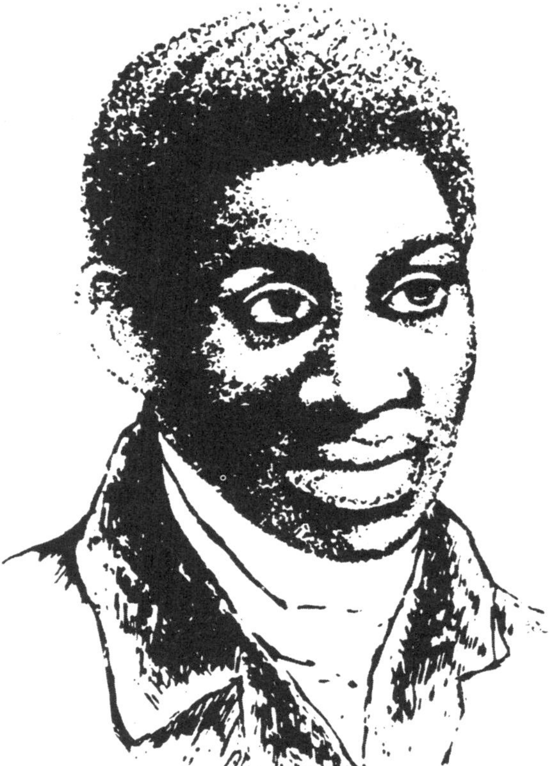

To Barbara
in love and gratitude

She is far more precious than jewels.
—*Proverbs 31:10 (RSV)*

CONTENTS

Preface   9
Foreword   11

Introduction   13
The Black Presence
Origins   18
Early Ministry with Asbury   21
Portrait of a Circuit Rider   24
Wesley's Emissary Arrives   28
The Christmas Conference   30
Hosier and Allen   33
Continued Travels   36
Garrettson's Ministry   39
Charges   46
Preachers Remember   48
Colbert and Hosier   52
The Question of Ordination   55
A Note of Sadness   57
Hosier's Death   59
Hosier's Ministry   61

Selected Bibliography   63

PREFACE

The Harry Hosier story must be told! Not only is it a vital factor in Methodist history, it becomes an integral chapter in the epic of America. His is more than the biography of an individual black man. Not only does Harry Hosier stand as a fascinating personality, he also represents an ethnic minority at a major junction in the evolving chronicle of both church and nation.

Harry Hosier's saga is the account of heroic faith, witness, and struggle set in the context of slavery and oppression. We encounter a dynamic personality who, by the grace of God, overcame seemingly insurmountable obstacles to rise as one of our foremost circuit riding preachers.

Gathering data on Harry Hosier has been a long—and exciting—process. His biography has been reconstructed from countless sources, including photocopy pages from a typed, unidentified paper which I have been unable to trace. In describing the life experiences of Harry Hosier, I have intentionally raised a number of intriguing questions regarding this extraordinary preacher. It is my hope that additional information—and answers—will be found as the search continues.

Bible quotations are from the King James Version. This translation could have been quoted by Harry Hosier.

Harry Hosier speaks to all of us, furnishing inspiration, insight, and fresh enthusiasm for a creative, contemporary evangelism: proclamation of the gospel of Jesus Christ.

WARREN THOMAS SMITH
The Interdenominational Theological Center
Atlanta, Georgia
May 18, 1980
The Anniversary of Harry Hosier's Funeral

FOREWORD

No account of the beginning and expansion of Methodism in America would be complete without including Harry"Black Harry" Hosier among its unsung pioneer preachers.

Harry became the most eloquent exhorter of his day. Those who heard him agree that he demonstrated unusual intellectual capacity, remarkable retention, and creative ability. He shared preaching opportunities with many proclaimers of the gospel including Asbury, Coke, Garrettson, Whatcoat, Boehm, Walker and Colbert. No singular personage of the Asburian period of Methodism espoused a more genuine biblical approach to the Methodist message or presented the cause of Christ more convincingly than Harry Hosier, traveling companion and servant-guide of Francis Asbury.

He was the one African of the eastern frontier who acted out with earnest devotion the urgent commission of John Wesley to his disciples . . ."I let you loose on the great continent of America. Publish your message in the open face of the sun and do all the good you can." Harry covered the Methodist itinerant from the Carolinas to New England, preaching the good news of salvation to all.

CIRCUIT RIDER

As the first ecumenical preacher of American Methodism, Hosier more than any other itinerant of his time, fused large interdenominational audiences through the gospel according to Methodism. He possessed the dynamic which dissolved the boundaries of separatism, making all one in Christ. His preaching partnership with Francis Asbury provided Methodism an outreach to the enslaved and the free, the poor and the rich, the churchless and the churchgoing.

> RALPH E. BLANKS, Pastor
> *Mother African Zoar United Methodist Church*
> *Philadelphia, PA 19123*

INTRODUCTION

The circuit rider stands as one of the major contributors—an outstanding contribution—to American church history, certainly to the Methodist phase of the story. Astride his horse, he traversed the frontier, bringing the gospel to an essentially untrodden, yet rapidly burgeoning America. There was a sense of pioneering, fresh beginnings. It was a land where new, sparsely populated settlements were springing up amid expanses of virgin forests, swamps, mountains, and river valleys. Did Europe know a comparable figure and a parallel situation? There, antiquity was ever in evidence; realization of a hoary past was inescapable. The traveling preacher in western Europe—Wesley is a good example—lived in a milieu wherein even evangelistic preaching was, for the most part, in settled, old communities. For America, in the late eighteenth and early nineteenth centuries, the wilderness was never ending: there was the log cabin, the small farm, the remote plantation, the isolated family. Cities were few, but growing in size. In 1790, Boston had a population of 18,038; New York was the largest with 33,131 citizens; Philadelphia with 28,522. Baltimore could boast 13,503. Washington, D. C.—or Washington City, as it was called—was just emerging from a dream by Thomas Jefferson and Alexander Hamilton. Charleston (including St.

Philip's and St. Michael's Parishes) had 16,359 and Savannah (along with Chatham County) 10,769. Villages and crossroads settlements dotted the largely rural Atlantic seaboard.

The church was on the move, represented by the circuit rider: keeping pace with the westward population march across the Appalachians; riding into hamlets where frequently no church existed; preaching on plantations in Maryland, Virginia, the Carolinas, and Georgia. He knew brush arbors, clapboard meetinghouses, country store porches, and clearings beside mountain streams. These were his preaching places.

THE BLACK PRESENCE

Booker T. Washington, in 1909, reflected thoughtfully and seriously about the rise from slavery. In *The Story of the Negro,* he surveyed the long, arduous struggle, and the part played by followers of John Wesley. "The Negro seems from the beginning to have been very closely associated with the Methodist Church in the United States," said Washington. He continued:

> Methodism had started in England among the poor and the outcast; it was natural, therefore, that when its missionaries came to America they should seek to bring into the Church the outcast and neglected people, especially the slaves.

Did Methodism have a special mission to black people? Washington said Methodists took it seriously:

> In some parts of the South the Methodist meetinghouses were referred to by the more aristocratic denominations as "the Negro churches." This was due to the fact that the Methodists often began their work in the community with an appeal to the slaves.

Washington then cited an example of this outreach: the preacher who accompanied Thomas Coke on several of his American tours,

HARRY HOSIER

Harry Hosier, a coloured minister who was at the same time the bishop's servant and an evangelist of the Church. . . . He travelled extensively through the New England and Southern states and shared the pulpits of the white ministers whom he accompanied. But he seems to have excelled them all in popularity as a preacher.

Harry Hosier was a circuit rider of the colonial-early national period in American life. It was also the tragic slave era, a backbreaking, heartbreaking, dehumanizing time. Caught in an inconceivable social situation, the black preacher proclaimed his message of hope to an oppressed people who would continue to suffer bondage as slaves for several more generations. He faced opposition in forms blatant and subtle. Any open attack by the preacher on the institution of slavery would put his ministry in jeopardy, for regardless of his personal status—slave or free—there was always the white master with whom he had to contend. Reprisals could be swift. Preaching, therefore, required prophetic honesty, courage, faithfulness to the gospel, and at the same time, tact and finesse when the slaveholder had his ear to the ground.

Only complete dedication to God's will and purpose could sustain Harry Hosier through all the vagaries of weather, tortuous trails along dense woodlands, inhospitable communities, and every physical ailment that might plague a weary traveler. He was a horseman for the Lord. His ministry takes on added importance and new perspective in that on his tours he preached quite as much to whites as to blacks. His was perhaps the first outstanding example of an inclusive ministry in American Methodism. It was no simple task, and only a preacher of remarkable talent would have been capable of such innovative and courageous undertakings.

Harry Hosier (spellings differ: *Hoosier, Hoshur, Hossier*) was known as "Black Harry." His story is as fascinating as it is mysterious. Most itinerant preachers of this time had little formal education; many were self-educated. Hosier was no exception; in fact, he could neither read nor write. We thus have no personal records from his hand—no letters, journals, sermons, or papers. All that we know comes either via oral tradition, legends and pious stories, or notes made—fortunately—by the few who knew him personally. Some writers secured information secondhand. These must all be sorted, then pieced together with care and understanding. Hosier's biography is filled with unresolved questions. It is a complicated maze through which we make our way, seeing him through others' eyes.

ORIGINS

It has been assumed that Harry Hosier was born near Fayetteville, North Carolina, about 1750. We have difficulty finding support for these claims. Originally Cumberland County was created out of Bladen County in 1754. The town was known as Cross Creek or Campbellton, and in 1783 named Fayetteville, in honor of Lafayette. We know nothing of Hosier's parents, their roots, where they came from. Africa, yes, but how many generations ago and from what area, what country? What of his name, and for whom named: his father, a relative, a planter? Do families of that name reside in the present city? "We find no record of the above stated name," says the Register of Deeds of Cumberland County. *The Story of Fayetteville* by John A. Oates does not mention Harry Hosier.

Henry Evans (c. 1740-1810), a well-remembered black preacher from Virginia, was responsible for the original Methodist congregation—the present Hay Street United Methodist Church—in Fayetteville. He came to the area about 1780. Some have suggested that Hosier was a member of Evans's church. If so, how well did these two black preachers know each other? There is universal agreement that Hosier was born a slave. Could he have been sold at the slave market which still stands in Fayetteville?

A thesis has been advanced that Hosier was the slave of the well-known Henry (Harry) Dorsey Gough (?-1808), owner of the lustrous plantation Perry Hall, twelve miles northeast of Baltimore, at the intersection of Harford Road and Big Gunpowder River. The home was said to be a most spacious and elegant building. Gough was wealthy, having inherited an estate from his English kin valued at more than three hundred thousand dollars.

Initially Gough was almost irreligious, but his aristocratic and affluent wife, Prudence, sister of Maryland's Governor Ridgeley, was a devout Methodist. In 1775, Francis Asbury preached nearby; Gough heard the sermon and told his wife, "I shall never hinder you again from hearing the Methodists." Gough himself later chanced to hear an old slave saying his prayers, was profoundly awakened, and exclaimed, "I have found the Methodists' blessing! I have found the Methodists' God!" On March 11, 1776, Asbury visited Perry Hall and solemnly observed, "May this family evidence that all things are possible with God; though their salvation should be attended with as much apparent difficulty as the passage of a camel through the eye of a needle! If they prove faithful stewards they will."

A chapel was erected at Perry Hall, a step often taken by slaveholders. Assuming Hosier lived there, would he have heard the bell (said to be the first in an American Methodist meetinghouse)? Would he have listened to the circuit preacher who visited twice a month, or other local preachers who filled in alternate Sundays? Was he present at Mrs. Gough's prayer meetings, singing heartily Charles Wesley's hymns and listening as the Bible was read? Was this his introduction to Wesleyan theology? Hosier is said to be the first African to be licensed to preach in American Methodism. Did he respond to an altar call, giving his life to Christ and his service to Methodism? Who preached? When was he baptized, and by whom? Or had this taken place in North Carolina?

At some point Harry Hosier was manumitted. By whom? Gough? The Henry Dorsey Gough papers—all of a purely business nature—make no mention of Harry Hosier. Did Hosier purchase his freedom, as did Richard Allen, who later founded the African Methodist Episcopal Church? If Hosier was born in North Carolina and was then taken to Maryland, did he ever return to Fayetteville? We know the Baltimore territory remained an important part of his ministry. We have no documentary proof establishing ties between the Goughs and Hosier, but the theory is plausible, even to the name: Harry. It would have been easy for Hosier to have met Asbury and other Methodist leaders at Perry Hall and a bond established.

EARLY MINISTRY WITH ASBURY

When did Harry Hosier and Francis Asbury (1745-1816) first meet? We can only speculate. As early as January 24, 1773, when Asbury was in Baltimore, he wrote his parents in England, "Poor Negroes have been deeply affected with the power of God. We have got one that will be fit to send to England soon, to preach." He went on, "Here are Negroes who have astonished masters of families, understanding men, when they have heard them pray; and if they were in England, they would shame their thousands."

Is this a possible reference to Harry Hosier? We cannot be certain, but if so it places an early date for the acquaintance of Asbury and Hosier and also gives credence to the theory that Hosier was in the Baltimore area, perhaps at Perry Hall. The year 1773 poses a question as to a possible tie between "astonished masters" and the Goughs. Did Asbury know the family at this early time? An intriguing query is, did the black preacher mentioned by Asbury ever go to England? Is it possible that Harry Hosier might have made such a trip?

Did Asbury and Hosier initially encounter each other during the 1775 preaching mission or the 1776 visit to Perry Hall? It is not possible to be sure. We have Asbury's first mention of Hosier on Thursday, June 29, 1780. On the previous day Asbury had gone to Todd's in North Carolina, near the Virginia line, and this brings Carolina back as the possible area of Hosier's origin. Asbury was contemplating an evangelistic campaign to reach the slaves. "I have thought if I had two horses, and Harry (a coloured man) to go with, and drive one, and meet the black people, and to spend about six months in Virginia, and the Carolinas, it would be attended with a blessing," he noted in his *Journal*.

A year passes, and we pick up the story at Fairfax Chapel in Falls Church, Virginia, on Sunday, May 13, 1781, where the two preached. Hearing a black was new: "the white people looked on with attention." Hosier used his familiar text—the exact reference unknown—relating to the barren fig tree. Perhaps the text might have been Matthew 21:19-21, or Mark 11:13-14, 21ff., the account of the one Jesus cursed, a dramatic vignette of faith, prayer, accountability, and discipleship. It may have been Luke 13:6-9, the account of the nonproductive tree in the vineyard, a parable which relates to judgment and repentance, to faith and patience, to caring and nurturing. Either text would seem an appropriate passage for Hosier to use. The barren fig tree was a favorite theme, repeated frequently, as was customary with circuit riders. Their repertoire was limited, but polished. Strong Methodist theology was evident at P. Hite's on Monday, May 21, when Hosier preached to the blacks who had come a considerable distance just to hear him. It was not a bland message, and "certain sectarians," noted Asbury, "are greatly displeased with him, because he tells them they may fall from grace, and that they must be holy." The "once in grace, always in grace" debate with Baptists was always popular.

The crisp autumn day of Saturday, October 27, 1781, found Asbury in Delaware, struggling to prepare an abridgment of Richard Baxter's *Cure for Church Divisions*. He was also planning a return to Virginia in the winter. Asbury noted somewhat grudgingly, "Harry seems to be unwilling to go with me: I fear his speaking so much to white people in the city has been, or will be, injurious; he has been flattered, and may be ruined."

PORTRAIT OF A CIRCUIT RIDER

Harry Hosier was popular with whites from the beginning. Asbury gives the impression their praise was fulsome, perhaps tinged with a pinch of sympathy. While this may have obtained in some cases, there were competent observers. What was the secret for such amazing skill? G. A. Raybold wrote in 1849, recalling that Richard Allen wanted to teach Harry Hosier to read, "but, to use Hosier's phrase, 'when he tried to read, he lost the gift of preaching,' and gave it up entirely." Hosier had an excellent memory:

> Harry could remember passages of Scripture and quote them accurately; and hymns, also, which he had heard read, he could repeat or sing. He was never at a loss in preaching, but was very acceptable wherever he went, and few of the white preachers could equal him, in his way.

Hosier possessed a master key: a resplendent tradition in black preaching.

> When he was questioned as to his preaching abilities, complete command of voice, aptness in language, and free delivery, as to Scripture and doctrinal truth, his reply was a description of the Elocution of Faith: "I sing

by faith, pray by faith, preach by faith, and do everything by faith; without faith in the Lord Jesus I can do nothing."

What of Hosier's preaching? Do we depend on sentimental traditions, embellished by time? Hardly! The noted Dr. Benjamin Rush (1745-1813), of Philadelphia—outstanding physician, member of the Continental Congress, signer of the Declaration of Independence, quizzical Presbyterian, practicing ecumenicist, personal friend of Benjamin Franklin, and pioneer abolitionist—heard Hosier and exclaimed, "Making allowances for his illiteracy he was the greatest orator in America." Raybold called Hosier "one of the greatest prodigies of those early days." G. A. Raybold also remembered what "the justly celebrated Dr. Sargent" (1776-1833), of Philadelphia, one of Methodism's "chiefs of the ministry," an able pulpiteer himself and a good judge of preaching, said of Black Harry. Raybold tells us Dr. Sargent pronounced Hosier "the greatest natural orator he ever heard." Harry Hosier's fame was widespread; he commanded large congregations and "his sermons were appreciated by audiences without distinction of color," said John Fletcher Hurst.

The Negro History Bulletin gives a penetrative analysis, "Black Harry also became a national figure as a companion preacher of Asbury." The preaching plan? "The white minister usually called on the Negro to move the audience with the awfulness of sin and judgment to come and the prospects for blessings from temperance and righteousness. Then the white minister would follow with a doctrinal discussion to accept the sheep in the fold." Was this true of Harry Hosier?

In most assemblies Hosier first spoke to the blacks. As the message progressed, whites joined the congregation. Did they come in a patronizing spirit? Possibly at first. The novelty of listening to a black, a former slave, would have attracted many. Hosier's power seemed to mesmerize; transcend all racial barriers. What of content? It was biblical—we have a number of texts which reveal depth and insight. Being unable to read or write, how did he study? It was not conventional learning from a text. His power of observation, his immense store of illustrations, his prodigious memory, his ability to concentrate—all gave him an enormous fund of resources.

"Black Harry" spent months with Asbury and other preachers. As they rode horseback there would have been ample time for conversation about the Bible, fundamental beliefs, the Christian life, prayer. At a camp meeting all preachers of the area would be on hand, taking turns at the rough, brush arbor pulpit. As they heard their brothers, they learned. It was frontier preaching, but let us not make the mistake of demeaning it. There may have been scant erudition, but there was brainpower aplenty (Asbury taught himself Hebrew). These circuit riders developed a finely honed homiletical style through repetition. True, the "holy whine"—that rather shrill intonation, interpreted as the working of the Holy Spirit—appeared now and then, much to the delight of some congregations. Hosier grasped ideas from his colleagues, and they learned from him, but they were unable to copy him. Above all, there would have been Hosier's own experience of grace; he had met Jesus Christ.

What of Harry Hosier's physical appearance? John Lednum quotes an old source, "He was small, very black, keen-eyed, possessing great volubility of tongue." There is an old cartoon which shows Hosier with Bible in hand, intently conversing with a spellbound listener. We have a line drawing of Hosier's kindly face, with special attention to his large, loving eyes. Virginia J. Kiah of Savannah, Georgia, has painted an oil portrait which now hangs in St. George's United Methodist Church in Philadelphia. W. P. Harrison, writing in 1893, used a familiar description:

> Harry was small in stature, coal black, and with eyes of remarkable brilliance and intelligence. He had a quick mind, a most retentive memory, and such an eloquent flow of words, which he could soon put into almost faultless English, that he was pronounced by many "The greatest orator in America."

Riding the circuit with Asbury provided Hosier a measure of freedom that the preacher assigned to a church would not have enjoyed. Like many circuit riders, he probably was not married and had no permanent home. There were distinct advantages: he was not confined, nor was he bound to the whims of a single congregation or plantation owner. Neither was he forced to prepare a fresh sermon each Sunday. Travel permitted a limited autonomy; he could pioneer into new territory as opportunity invited. He was young, strong, and a man of growing importance.

WESLEY'S EMISSARY ARRIVES

Thomas Coke (1747-1814) came to America as John Wesley's representative. Born in Wales and educated at Oxford, Coke was regarded as one of Methodism's best preachers. Asbury met the "Little Doctor" in a soul-stirring scene at Barratt's Chapel in Delaware on November 14, 1784. Harry Hosier, we are sure, was present. Asbury needed his expertise, not so much as preacher but as guide. Asbury wisely thought Coke needed a taste of frontier life, so he planned a "route of about eight hundred or a thousand miles" as a preaching tour through Delaware, Maryland, and Virginia. Hosier had the dubious pleasure of guiding the noted Oxonian. It might have been a dismal chore. "He has given me his black (*Harry* by name) and borrowed an excellent horse for me," Dr. Coke wrote in his *Journal*. From the outset "Black Harry" won the heart of Coke, who wrote on November 29, 1784:

> I have now had the pleasure of hearing *Harry* preach several times. I sometimes give notice immediately after preaching, that in a little time *Harry* will preach to the blacks; but the whites always stay to hear him. Sometimes I publish him to preach at candle-light, as the Negroes can better attend at that time.

Coke then gave his assessment of Harry Hosier, "I really believe he is one of the best Preachers in the world, there is such an amazing power attends his preaching, though he cannot read; and he is one of the humblest creatures I ever saw." A skilled preacher can recognize another skilled preacher!

Some days later, Monday, December 6, the Welshman acknowledged profound gratitude for Hosier's common sense.

> I had this morning a great escape in crossing a broad ferry. After setting off, *Harry* persuaded me to return back, and leave our horses behind us, to be sent after me the next day, on account of the violence of the wind. I have hardly a doubt but we should have been drowned if we had not taken that step. We were in great danger as it was.

The tour was important, both for personal friendship and prophetic vision. Coke was to become champion of a brief but important antislavery campaign in America. Could he have discovered the reality of American slavery from Harry Hosier? There would have been opportunity for free expression—man to man. It is possible that Coke realized the need while sharing the lonely vigil with Hosier.

THE CHRISTMAS CONFERENCE

Methodism, as a formal organization, was about to take shape. The tour concluded at Abingdon, Maryland, where Coke met Asbury. Plans for Baltimore were in the offing. The men journeyed to Perry Hall on Friday, December 17, to chart the course of the forthcoming assembly. Hosier most certainly would have been with the preachers who spent more than a week at Perry Hall, but we have no documentation.

The Christmas Conference assembled in Baltimore, at Lovely Lane Chapel, meeting from December 24, 1784, until January 2, 1785. The Methodist Episcopal Church was born at this notable gathering. Harry Hosier and Richard Allen (1760-1831)—later to be designated first Bishop of the African Methodist Episcopal Church—would surely have been in the audience. George A. Singleton tells us:

> When the historic Christmas Conference met at Baltimore in 1784 to carry out John Wesley's plan to organize Methodism in the colonies, two Negro preachers were present: Richard Allen and "Black Harry," whose real name was Harry Hoosier. He had traveled with Thomas Coke and Asbury, and the former regarded him "as one of the best preachers in the world."

It is intriguing to imagine Harry Hosier watching the proceedings, as Coke presided, and read the *Circular Letter* from Wesley. Asbury was ordained deacon on Christmas

Day, elder on December 26, and on December 27 was set apart as superintendent by Coke, assisted by Thomas Vasey (c. 1746-1826); Richard Whatcoat (1736-1806), who had accompanied Coke to America; and Philip William Otterbein (1726-1813) of the German Evangelical Reformed Church. Hosier would have known all these men, some as familiar friends. Others, Vasey and Otterbein, he probably knew casually. Hosier belonged at the Conference. He very likely took no part, but remained quietly in the background.

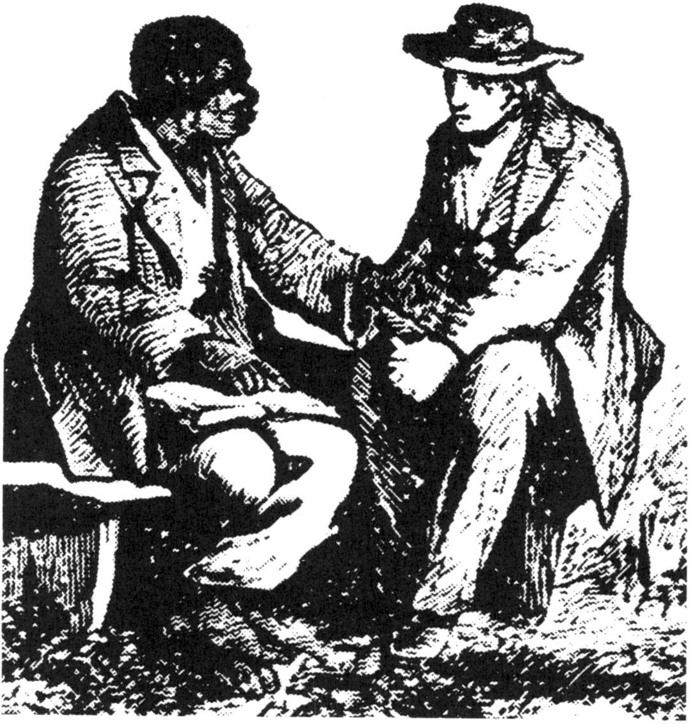

HOSIER AND ALLEN

The two blacks, Harry Hosier and Richard Allen, represent appealing contrasts in personality. Allen had no comment about Hosier in his *Life Experiences;* it is regrettable. Personal relationships, shared by the two, would make enjoyable reading and important observations. It is obvious they were not the intimate companions that Allen and Absalom Jones (1746-1818) were.

Allen "worked with his hands for his own support as he preached" just as Paul had done. Allen had a prophet's scorn of slavery. After the unhappy experience at St. George's Church in Philadelphia, he and Jones declared their independence. The Free African Society was one example. Did Harry Hosier ever become a member? Allen became founder of the African Methodist Episcopal Church and Jones the first black to be ordained in the Episcopal Church. Hosier, on the other hand, remained a preacher in the predominantly white Methodist Episcopal Church.

Hosier and Asbury got along quite well, sharing the long road together. With Allen, it was another matter, and he described the conversation candidly: "Rev. Bishop Asbury sent for me to meet him at Henry Gaff's. I did so. He told me he wished me to travel with him." There were certain provisions, however. "He told me that in the slave countries, Carolina and other places, I must not intermix with the slaves, and I would frequently have to sleep in his carriage, and he would allow me my victuals and clothes." Allen saw things differently:

> I told him I would not travel with him on these conditions. He asked me my reasons. I told him if I was taken sick, who was to support me? and that I thought people ought to lay up something while they were able, to support themselves in time of sickness or old age.

Asbury responded with equal honesty and firmness. "He said that was as much as he got, his victuals and clothes." Allen continued, "I told him he would be taken care of, let his afflictions be as they were, or let him be taken sick where he would, he would be taken care of; but I doubted whether it would be the case with myself." The conversation concluded, "He smiled, and told me he would give me from then until he returned from the eastward to make up my mind, which would be about three months. But I made up my mind that I would not accept of his proposals." The two remained friends and their association continued during coming years, but Allen was never the traveling companion of Asbury that Hosier was.

We see in Allen another approach to ministry—and a different temperament. Both Hosier and Allen had known slavery personally. They were now free men. Why did Hosier not stand toe to toe with Asbury? He may have done so intrepidly, and we have no record. It would appear, however, that Hosier's gentle personality called for another stance. Did he respond to his social situation by acquiescing to the white majority? Did he find it comfortable and profitable? It is difficult to think so. In the final analysis it seems clear that Harry Hosier, a man of gracious spirit and charitable disposition, chose of his own free will to be part of his Methodist Episcopal Church, living out his life as one of its ministering members.

CONTINUED TRAVELS

In Wilmington, Delaware, so the oft-told story runs, Asbury and Hosier came for preaching services at Old Asbury Chapel. Methodism was unpopular in the community, nonetheless an overflow crowd gathered, many standing outside listening through the open windows. A participant affirmed, "If all Methodist preachers could preach like the bishop, we should like to be constant hearers." Another responded, "That is not the bishop, but the bishop's servant that you heard." The reply was immediate, "If such be the servant, what must the master be?" According to Lednum, "The truth was, that Harry was a more popular speaker than Mr. Asbury, or almost anyone else in his day." Hosier had a silver tongue, but what of speech patterns? Could he have possessed a British—or trace of British—accent? The same question applied to Asbury, English by birth and a resident until he was twenty-six.

In the early autumn of 1786, Hosier accompanied Asbury to New York. Hosier delivered his first New York sermon at the John Street Church in September. The *New York Packet* of September 11, 1786, gave a detailed write-up (the first time notice was given to Methodist preaching in any of the city's newspapers): "Lately came to this city a very singular black man, who, it is said, is quite ignorant of letters, yet he has preached in the Methodist church several times to the acceptance of several well-disposed, judicious people." The story went on:

> He delivers his discourses with great zeal and pathos, and his language and connection is by no means contemptible. It is the wish of several of our correspondents that this same black man may be so far successful as to rouse the dormant zeal of members of our slothful white people, who seem very little affected about concerns of another world.

In order to help with his travel, the John Street people collected two pounds for use, carefully listing the contribution in the *John Street Church Records*.

In May of 1787, Thomas Coke was engaged in another of his nine American visits. Hosier and Asbury rode with him from Baltimore to New York. Once more, on June 11, Hosier was given the sum of two pounds—apparently a standard travel expenditure. This trip appears to be the concluding tour with both Coke and Asbury. They had covered many miles together; there were never-to-be-forgotten adventures, but sadly enough, no one recorded them and they are forgotten. History is the poorer for it.

That same year, 1787, the Methodist Episcopal Church asked a disciplinary question: *"What direction shall we give for the promotion of the spiritual welfare of the coloured people?"* The answer was direct; the *Minutes* report:

> We conjure all our Ministers and Preachers by the love of God, and the salvation of souls, and do require them, by all the authority that is invested in us, to leave nothing

undone for the spiritual benefit and salvation of them, within their respective circuits, or districts; and for this purpose to embrace every opportunity of inquiring into the state of their souls, and to unite in society those who appear to have a real desire of fleeing from the wrath to come, to meet such in class, and to exercise the whole discipline among them.

We cannot be sure of Hosier's possible influence with church leaders, but his physical presence would have been a constant reminder of the black membership and the obligation to provide an adequate ministry.

Hosier toured with Richard Whatcoat during 1786-1788, the time Whatcoat served as Presiding Elder in Delaware, Eastern Maryland, and Eastern Pennsylvania. Whatcoat reported an impressive gain of 847 Negro members in the three charges under his supervision for 1787. Undoubtedly Harry Hosier should be given credit for much of this increase.

At Duck Creek, Delaware, Whatcoat and Hosier held services in the Friends Meetinghouse. Sermons by the two were "long remembered" by folk in the community. In 1800, Whatcoat was elected the third bishop in the Methodist Episcopal Church, following Coke and Asbury. This means Harry Hosier, personal friend of all three, knew them as perhaps no other individual could. What priceless stories he could have told—of tears and laughter—as these men journeyed together!

GARRETTSON'S MINISTRY

One of the most remarkable phases of Harry Hosier's life came through association with Freeborn Garrettson (1752-1827), a Marylander by birth who knew the Susquehanna River area from childhood. His conversion, as he told it in his *Narrative,* was wondrous, and centered on the sinfulness of slavery. He described the service, "While I was giving out a hymn, this thought powerfully struck my mind. *'It is not right for you to keep your Fellow-Creatures in Bondage! You must let the oppressed go free.'* " He was absolutely sure of the directive, "I knew this was the voice of the Lord." He continued:

> Till this moment, I never suspected that the practice of Slave-keeping was wrong; having neither read any thing on the subject; nor conversed with persons respecting its sinfulness. After a minute's pause, I replied, "Lord, the oppressed shall go free."

Garrettson then turned, and "addressed the Slaves, and told them, 'You do not belong to me: I will not desire your service without making you a significant compensation.' " He later affirmed it "was God, and not man, that taught me the impropriety of holding slaves: and I shall never be able to praise him enough for it." He then commented,

"My very heart bleeds for Slave-holders, especially those who make a profession of Religion."

Garrettson's concern for slaves became a vital part of his ministry. "In September 1777, I traveled in Roanoak Circuit, North Carolina. The cruelties which the poor Negroes suffered affected me greatly." He then described his preaching method:

> I endeavoured frequently to inculcate the doctrine of Freedom, in a private way, which procured me the displeasure of some interested persons. I set apart times to preach to the Blacks, and adapted my discourse to their capacity; these were refreshing seasons from [i.e., because of] the presence of the Lord: Often were their sable faces overflowed with penitential tears, while their hands of faith were stretched out to embrace Salvation through Jesus Christ.

He concluded his rather dramatic account, "Their captivity and sufferings were sanctified, and drove them to the Friend of sinners; many of them were exceedingly happy, through the manifestations of pardoning mercy."

It is easy to see that Garrettson would have had an affinity with Hosier. We wonder why there was no mention of "Black Harry" by Garrettson at the 1784 meeting at Barratt's Chapel. Both men were present. Garrettson, however, makes scant reference to any individual. Once Garrettson and Hosier became a team in 1789, their travels provide insightful data. At that time Garrettson had charge of Methodist work in New York, extending from the Hudson River to Schenectady and eastward into New England. He was a dynamo and sought out potential members aggressively. Coke described, with glee, the advance made in 1789: *"Freeborn Garrettson,* one of our Presiding Elders, has been greatly blessed; and is endued with an uncommon talent for opening new places . . . The numbers in the State of *New-York,* are 2,004; the increase 900." Coke went on, proudly telling of Methodist growth, "The whole number in the United States, is 43,265: the whole increase, 6,111: . . . of the above-mentioned number, 35,021 are White, 8,241 are Blacks, and three are Indians."

The summer of 1790 stands as one of the brightest chapters in Hosier's career. He and Garrettson made a tour of New England. Leaving New York on June 2 they journeyed north. Garrettson carefully mapped out their itinerary, noting he was "accompanied by Harry, who is to travel with me this summer." They rode to "Mile's Square [New York], and preached to more people than could get into the house." June 5 found them in King Street where "Harry exhorted after me to the admiration of the people." It was the same on Tuesday, June 8, a "joyful season" and the "people of this circuit were amazingly fond of hearing Harry." June 10 was a day of rain but people came for morning preaching and in the afternoon "the old English Church" was almost filled. Garrettson proclaimed, "He that is born of God doth not commit sin." Hosier preached next and, strangely, "it was a heavy cross" for him. On the following Monday, people came from all parts of Oswego, New York, to hear Hosier—some out of sheer curiosity.

The two evangelists went on to Connecticut, and on Saturday, June 19, there was preaching at Mr. Herricks. "Harry exhorted after me with much freedom." It was glorious. St. Michael's Episcopal Church was open for them at Litchfield the following Wednesday, June 23. Garrettson preached, then departed for the center of town, to the "old church on the Green," leaving Hosier to deliver a sermon to the congregation which remained to hear him. Hartford was reached on June 28 and between five and six hundred people assembled at the courthouse. Sadly, "while Harry gave an exhortation some rude people behaved very uncivilly." These moments appeared along with the triumphs; it was, woefully, part of life. Racial prejudice, along with boorishness, can find its way into many otherwise happy situations.

They arrived in Boston on Tuesday, July 1. Garrettson made arrangements, "I boarded Harry with the master mason for the Africans." This would have been the well-known Prince Hall (1735-1807) who founded the first Masonic Lodge for Africans: the Prince Hall Masonic Order. He had become a Methodist in 1774. The two would have had much to talk about. Did Harry Hosier become a Mason? Probably. Prince Hall stands as a leading citizen of Boston and the United States. His contribution to American life is noteworthy.

The stay in Boston was brief, and the evangelists were soon on their way south, moving toward Providence, Rhode Island. Meanwhile in Providence, Jesse Lee (1758-1816) had been preaching several times in the courthouse and at a private dwelling. As he was leaving, going north toward Boston, about ten miles out of town he saw two travelers coming toward him. "One of these horsemen was an intelligent but humble-looking colored man, who seemed to enjoy his position more than if he were attend-

CIRCUIT RIDER

ing a hero in a triumph," said Abel Stevens. To be sure, the "colored companion was the well known 'Black Harry,' who not only ministered to the temporal convenience of his master, but aided in his spiritual labors by frequently exhorting and preaching after him." This may have been the meeting in which Garrettson urged Lee to preach for a period of time in Boston in order to establish Methodism in New England. Lee did just that. He became the "founder" of Methodism in those beautiful states, and Harry Hosier was to work with him. These plans for the future may have been initiated there at the roadside.

Garrettson and Hosier went on to Providence and preached in "good old Mr. Snow's meeting house." Sunday, July 11, at six in the evening, Hosier preached to more than a thousand people. Sunday, July 25, the men were at Canaan, Connecticut, and Hosier's congregation numbered five hundred. It was a hot day and the service was held outside. The warmth of the sun was equalled by that of the people who loudly applauded the message. The meeting at Salisbury was "tender" and the weeping copious as Hosier exhorted. On Wednesday, July 28, Garrettson sent Hosier on to supply for him at an afternoon service. On the next day the team was at Hudson, New York, where Garrettson noted, "I found the people very curious to hear Harry. I therefore declined preaching that their curiosity might be satisfied. The different denominations heard him with much admiration, and the Quakers thought that as he was unlearned he must preach by immediate inspiration." Word was out: hear Harry Hosier! The impact of his message must have been tremendous. Hosier was now at the height of his career—about forty years of age and established as a noted evangelist. He was a liberated man preaching a liberating Gospel.

Freeborn Garrettson's far-ranging ministry included work in Canada. Did Hosier accompany him there? It has been suggested that Harry Hosier traveled as far northeast as Nova Scotia.

What was the relationship of Asbury, Coke, Whatcoat, and Garrettson to Harry Hosier? Affable paternalism? Probably—at least in the beginning. Francis Asbury took a fatherly view toward most of his preachers—black or white. As time passed, however, the climate appears to have changed, and many Methodists recognized the gifted evangelist. We must be careful not to paint an unreal picture. Elevated though he may have been, Hosier never seems to have stood on exactly the same footing with the others. Writers of mid- and late-nineteenth century described Hosier as *servant, traveling companion, guide* and *driver* as well as *preacher.* Nonetheless, a great many church people experienced genuine brotherhood.

A concern for blacks was best expressed in the question raised in 1790 for Methodist clergy: "What can be done in order to instruct poor children, white and black, to read?" Charles C. Jones tells us the answer: "Let us labor as the heart and soul of one man to establish Sunday schools in or near the places of public worship." Instructions were given to the preachers:

> Let persons be appointed by the bishops, elders, deacons, or preachers, to teach gratis all that will attend and have a capacity to learn, from 6 o'clock in the morning till 10, and from 2 P. M. till 6, where it does not

> interfere with public worship. This council shall compile a proper school-book to teach them learning and piety.

Stating that progress was made, and the effort was an honest one, Jones continues, "The Methodist is the only denomination which has preserved returns of the number of colored members in its connection." Blacks were part of the church. "Methodists met with more success during this period in the Middle and Southern States than in the Northern, and as they paid particular attention to the Negroes large numbers were brought under their influence."

CHARGES

Unhappily, clouds appeared in a bright sky. Accusations were made against Harry Hosier by Sally Lyon in 1791. The exact nature is not known. Was it misbehavior? Hosier would not be the first victim of a plot to embroil a noted preacher in scandal. Fortunately a full hearing was held:

Sally Lyon
  agt.
Henry Hosier

We the under named Subscribers having deliberately heard the Evidence on the part of the said Sally Lyon as well as that the part of said Henry Hosier, and according to said Evidence the Charge against the said Henry Hosier we have severally agreed he is not guilty.

Northcastle
Oct. 15th 1791

James McDonald, Rev. Isaac Foster, Gilbert Thorn, Thomas Sands, John Ferris, Charles Brundige, Squire Dann, Abraham Hart, Isaac Smith.

This Certifies that the above is a true copy from the Original report taken by us. Thomas Morrell—Elder
                      Jacob Brush   —Elder

Justice was done and Hosier's good name was cleared.

Thomas Morrell (1747-1838), leading Methodist preacher who served major churches in New York, Philadelphia, Baltimore, and Charleston, preserved the original report. It now belongs to Garrett-Evangelical Theological Seminary as part of the "The Morrell Collection" housed in the Library.

PREACHERS REMEMBER

Several preachers wrote their reminiscences of Harry Hosier. Most of these men, younger than Hosier, knew him in his later years. They recalled situations of high drama which they enjoyed telling—and possibly embellished. Henry Boehm (1775-1875), born in Lancaster County, Pennsylvania, was a son of the illustrious Bishop Martin Boehm of the United Brethren in Christ. Henry was self-educated and as an itinerant preacher served primarily German-speaking Methodists in Maryland, Virginia, and Pennsylvania. He spent at least five and possibly as many as ten years traveling with Asbury. Boehm preached until the time of his death at the ripe old age of one hundred. He remembered Hosier clearly and happily.

As a young man, Boehm attended the Philadelphia Conference of 1803; his enthusiasm was unbounded, as recorded in his *Reminiscences*, "I heard, during the session, a number of admirable sermons: . . . I also heard "Black Harry,' who traveled with Bishop Asbury and Freeborn Garrettson." Boehm continued, with relish, describing Hosier. "He was a perfect character; could neither read nor write, and yet was very eloquent. His text was, 'Man goeth to his long home.' " This passage from Ecclesiastes 12:5 sounded a somber note:

> Also when they shall be afraid of that which is high, and fears shall be in the way, and the almond tree shall

flourish, and the grasshopper shall be a burden, and desire shall fail: because man goeth to his long home, and the mourners go about the streets.

But young Boehm was impressed—and he overworked *eloquent* in telling the story—Hosier's "sermon was one of great eloquence and power." By 1803, was the strain of years seen in Hosier's preaching? Members of the Conference did not think so, for the "preachers listened to this son of Ham with great wonder, attention and prophet [sic]."

Boehm, anxious to "say something more concerning him," told of the incongruous questions raised about Hosier. "Having heard this African preach, I have been asked a great many questions concerning him. The preaching of a colored man was, in those days, a novelty." Crowds had flocked to hear him during his travels with Asbury, Coke, and others "not only because he was a colored man, but because he was eloquent. Mr. Asbury wished him to travel with him for the benefit of the colored people." Alas, "Some inquired whether he was really black, or whether Anglo-Saxon blood was not mixed in his veins?" Boehm gave an instant reply. "Harry was very black, an African of the Africans." Boehm continued, telling of Hosier's illiteracy which prevented his reading a single word, but, oh, he could recite the lines of a hymn from memory, as though reading the page, and scripture texts were quoted with utmost accuracy. His voice was pure music and his tongue" as the pen of a ready writer." Boehm summed up Hosier's ministry, "He was unboundedly popular, and many would rather hear him than the bishops." The narrative concluded with a glowing account of travels with Garrettson and additional descriptions of Hosier's preaching—with echoes from Rush and Coke. Boehm was enthralled!

George A. Raybold (1802-1876), member of the New Jersey Conference, would not have known Hosier personally, but he talked with those who did. He called Hosier's entire life "a most extraordinary affair." Hosier was one who had been a slave in the southland, then set free, converted, and had become an evangelist for Jesus Christ. Raybold pointed out the pioneering: "Harry flourished long before Bishop Allen, of Philadelphia, had established his African Methodist Episcopal Church." Hosier and Asbury had actually "preached alternately" in a number of states, especially in Pennsylvania and New Jersey. How remarkable! It just was not done—a white and a black preaching *together*. All these wonders Raybold carefully recorded in *Reminiscences*.

Raybold told of Hosier's being assigned to the Trenton Circuit in 1803 "in company with" John Walker (1764-1849), who recalled a highly charged situation:

> On one occasion, at an appointment at Hackettstown, there was a lady in the house where the preachers stayed who declared "she would not hear the black." Harry heard it, and retired into a corner of the garden, and prayed in great fervour, until the hour of meeting.

The service, in a private home, was in Walker's hands. He delivered the sermon and Hosier sat quietly in a chair directly in front of the speaker. Raybold continued:

> At the conclusion of the sermon, Harry arose, stood behind the chair, and began, in the most humble manner, to speak of sin as a disease; all were affected there, and the Lord had sent a remedy by the hands of a physician; but, alas! he was black! and some might reject the only means of cure, because of the hands by which it was sent to them that day.

Hosier logically built his theme, "He went on in the same strain, until all hearts were moved; then he prayed, (few had the gift of prayer as had Black Harry; he was like Bishop Asbury in this respect—awful, powerful, and overwhelming!)." The moment had come for the traditional altar call—to the mourner's bench—and "a great time" it was. The "lady was cut to the heart, and speedily converted, as were many others, on that memorable occasion."

Hosier's kindness, patience, and sheer Christian love became increasingly evident. Raybold gave a word profile, "At that time Harry was becoming old, and his head grey." Hosier would have been about fifty-three; years and burdens had aged him. It is also possible that he was born prior to 1750.

> He was of middling stature; slim but very strongly built, and very black; capable of great labour and much endurance. He also possessed a most musical voice, which he could modulate with the skill of a master, and use with most complete success in the pathetic, terrible, or persuasive parts of a discourse.

COLBERT AND HOSIER

William Colbert (1764-1835) preached in Maryland, Delaware, New Jersey, Pennsylvania, and New York, and served for some years as Presiding Elder. His unpublished *Journal* portrays Hosier during the latter two and a half years of his ministry. It is illuminating, in spite of weird spellings of Hosier's name and assorted forms of punctuation. A lasting friendship was established. In Maryland, on Saturday, September 15, 1804, Colbert described a glorious Methodist tradition: "This forenoon . . . at our Camp meeting we had about 100 people . . . Henry Hoshur gave a powerful exhortation." The following day was even more successful, "This forenoon I suppose we had 1500 people . . . bro. Cooper gave an excellent and lengthy discourse from Matt. 24 ch. 14 v. after Harry Hoshur spoke from Matt. 6 ch. 10 v." It was the beloved, "Thy kingdom come. Thy will be done in earth, as it is in heaven." Camp meeting had a flavor and significance all its own, and Harry Hosier was part of it.

Some four months later Colbert was in Pennsylvania, and on Saturday, January 19, 1805, took part in another Methodist tradition. "Our Quarterly meeting began at Centerville . . . at night Thos Smith preached for us. . . . Henry Hosure a black man spoke after him with life and power." Colbert continued, depicting yet another Methodist institution: "We had a joyful season this morning in the Love-feast: both whites and blacks spoke with wisdom from above and animation." Colbert could hardly restrain himself. He noted, "At night Hanry Hoshure a black man; commonly call [sic] Black Harvy gave us an excellent discourse from Rev. 3rd ch. 20th v." The passage is the familiar, "Behold, I stand at the door, and knock: If any man hear my voice, and open the door, I will come in to him, and will sup with him, and he with me." Colbert concluded with perhaps the highest praise he could summon, "This is not a man made preacher. It is really surprising to hear a man that cannot read, preach like this man."

It was a few weeks later that Colbert noted, on Wednesday, February 6, 1805, "We were invited to dine at Thomas Battens, where we spent the afternoon, and at night heard Henry Hersure a black friend preach from Isaiah 3 ch 10 v." The quotation is, "Say ye to the righteous, that it shall be well with him: for they shall eat the fruit of their doings." Said Colbert, "The people were affected. I spoke after him, and concluded the Meeting. We lodged at James Batten."

Colbert recorded that he and Hosier were in Philadelphia on Tuesday, February 19, and "preached at St. Georges . . . Henry Hosure a black man gave a powerful exhortation after me." Two days later they left Philadelphia and rode to Germantown. There Colbert preached at night. "This meeting was appointed for Henry Hosure, who on some account did not attend." In making the trip from Wilmington to Baltimore on March 26 Colbert mentioned, "This forenoon I started with Alward White and Henry Hosure, a black preacher."

Philadelphia assumed increased importance in Harry

Hosier's ministry. He is credited with helping in the founding of Zoar Church—African Zoar Methodist Episcopal Church—said to be the "oldest Negro congregation" in the denomination. Asbury, on Thursday, August 4, 1796, recorded opening the new house of worship, but made no mention of Harry Hosier. Philadelphia played an important role in the struggle for freedom by black people.

THE QUESTION OF ORDINATION

Was Harry Hosier ordained? Colbert is probably responsible for drawing up a formal request—the document is now in the Archives of St. George's Church—signed by nineteen preachers of the Philadelphia Conference, petitioning the Bishops and the Conference, which was slated to meet in Chestertown, Maryland, on May 1, 1805. It is possibly a request for Hosier's ordination, but no specific mention is made of ministerial orders.

> The Preachers recommendations   May 1, 1805
> Henry Hosure
> African
> To the Bishops and conference of the Methodist Episcopal Church to assemble in Chestertown the 1st May 1805
>
> Dear Brethren,
>   We your brethren the official members of the Methodist Church in St. George in Philadelphia Believe Henry Hosure an African, a man that would be very useful if the Bishops and Conference in their wisdom could without establishing a bad precedent direct him
>
> William Colbert, W. Bishop, John Davis, William Fox, Hugh Macurdy, A. K. M'Caskey, Thos. Branagan, John

Woolson, Hugh Smith, Daniel McCurdy, John Jones, Jacob Lamb, Daniel Doughty, Alexander Cook, John McCurdy, Jacob Bechtel, Jacob Knows, John Andrews, David Abbott.

We have no proof that Harry Hosier was ever ordained. Asbury did ordain Richard Allen a deacon on June 11, 1799. Jesse Lee, in his *History of the Methodists,* maintains that Allen thus became "the first coloured man that was ever ordained by the Methodists in the United States." He added, "Several others have since been ordained in New-York and Philadelphia, and one from Lynchburg, Virginia." To awaken his fellow Methodists he urged, "As the rule has not been known in general among our preachers, I have thought it proper to give it this publication." In 1800, legislation was passed permitting ordination of blacks. Why was Hosier excluded? The recommendation from the nineteen preachers named on the petition was dated 1805. It would seem that of all people, Harry Hosier merited full clergy rights.

A NOTE OF SADNESS

One explanation for no ordination may be that Hosier is said to "have fallen from grace" and become an alcoholic. The old story runs, "He fell by wine, one of the strong enemies of both ministers and people." Said Lednum, "Now, alas! this popular preacher was a drunken rag-picker in the streets of Philadelphia." And he had once moved on "a tide of popularity for a number of years."

Boehm offered a ready reason,

> 'Tis painful to mar a picture so beautiful. Gladly I will leave it as it is. But, alas! poor Harry was so petted and made so much of that he became lifted up. Falling under the influence of strong drink, he made shipwreck of the faith, and for years he remained in this condition.

The comment "for years" is questionable in light of Hosier's activity as late as 1805, enchanting audiences with his preaching. Hosier's condition—and it may have been a nervous breakdown—is more likely to have been a matter of months in duration. Is it possible that his disappointment at not being ordained caused his problem? Boehm happily concludes, "He was afterwards reclaimed, and died in peace in Philadelphia."

Lednum provides a joyful denouement. On a particular

evening, Hosier started down the Neck, below Southwark, "determined to remain there until his backslidings were healed." Under a tree he wrestled, and like Jacob, was triumphant. His former power in preaching seems to have dissipated, but he continued as a faithful disciple. He "finished his course; and, it is believed, made a good end."

HOSIER'S DEATH

William Colbert was in Philadelphia on March 22, 1806, and noted with considerable feeling that he "believed Hosier to be in favour with God." Colbert was again in Philadelphia on Wednesday, April 30, 1806, and penned, "At night I visited Henry Hosure an old Black happy in the Lord and to appear with in but a few days of eternity." Hosier would have been about fifty-six at this time. The following night an exhausted Colbert wrote, "This day has been a day of disappointments to me. I got me a creature, and set off on a journey to Baltimore but had to return in consequence of her being so lame. This afternoon I visited Henry Hosure who appears to be but for a short time for this world but happy in God." Colbert was deeply moved by Harry Hosier's story and is said to have commented, "I was very much affected at some of the experiences of Harry Hosier which he in private conversation related." Who now cared for Hosier; did he now have family ties?

Harry Hosier died in Philadelphia, and was taken, it is said, to Palmer Burying Ground, a free cemetery in Kensington. On Sunday, May 18, 1806, William Colbert sadly made this entry in his *Journal,* "This morning preached at Kensington from 1 Thes. 5 ch. 19th v. and in the afternoon heard Christopher Adkinson a black man preach the funeral of Henry Hosure another Black man, from Tim. 2nd 4 ch 7, 8th."

> I have fought a good fight, I have finished my course, I have kept the faith: henceforth there is laid up for me a crown of righteousness, which the Lord, the righteous judge, shall give me at that day: and not to me only, but unto all them also that love his appearing.

Colbert said of Atkinson, "He was very broken but he made out better than I expected." Another eulogist was present. "Jeffry Budd spoke after him, and he spoke well—the people were affected." We are told "a large crowd of white and black" followed Hosier's body to its resting place.

Although some writers have placed Hosier's death at 1810, William Colbert's account is decisive in determining the correct date as being 1806.

Hosier's grave cannot be located in the designated cemetery. It is possible we have confusion as to the location. Raybold concluded that Harry Hosier "died in Philadelphia, and was buried in the ground attached to Old Zoar," which is in contrast to the Kensington site. Raybold described the funeral, "on which occasion the late Jeffrey Bewley, a coloured preacher, and himself a wonder for capacity and performance, in eulogizing Black Harry, applied a term by which he was well known: 'Here lies the African wonder.' " Perhaps it is the perfect epitaph.

Raybold added: "Harry was, indeed, a wonder of grace, a wonder as a gifted minister of the gospel; all things considered, he was the greatest wonder or prodigy of the kind that had ever appeared before, whatever education and religion may have produced since his day."

HOSIER'S MINISTRY

There is no question that Harry Hosier was a rhetorician of remarkable skill. Asbury was assured of a good congregation if "Black Harry" was to preach with him. *The Negro History Bulletin* commented:

> The fact was that at that time there were few preachers in America who could compete with Black Harry. The high and low heard him with great satisfaction and acknowledged his unusual gift for evangelism in the then backward America. Historians of unbiased circles still pay him tribute as one of the great pioneer preachers of America.

He stands as one of Methodism's most extraordinary preachers. Booker T. Washington said that Harry Hosier was "the first American Negro preacher of the Methodist Church in the United States, . . . one of the notable characters of his day."

Methodism did make gains in its ministry to Negroes. Statistics show, "In 1786 there were 1,890 colored Methodists in America. By 1790 this number had increased to 11,682. From 1790 to 1810 one fifth of the membership of the Methodist Episcopal Church consisted of Negroes." This reflects Hosier's work. Yet more, every membership gain reflected his ministry, for he preached to all. He had a large following. His popularity may pose questions of identity. Did admiring parents name their children after him, thus resulting in duplication of names? He was loved and admired.

In seeking to evaluate Harry Hosier's life and work we cannot overlook the romanticism of the late nineteenth century. L. M. Hagood wrote, "White Bishop Asbury declared the truth as it is in Christ Jesus," and "black Harry by his side preached the same gospel." The goal was clear: sinners were saved "when black Harry pointed . . . to the cross." W. P. Harrison's portrait of the preacher said:

> The Methodist itinerants, having their hearts aglow with the pure missionary fire, preached at *all* alike. "Christ came into the world to die for *every* sinner," were the broad and liberal words emblazoned upon their shields. Everywhere that Methodist went, it went in that spirit. It was the religion for the rich and the poor, for the black and the white, for the master and slave; in short, for *all*.

Black Ministers of the Central Texas Conference of the United Methodist Church celebrated "The Harry Hosier Religious Extravaganza" Friday and Saturday, September 30-October 1, 1977. Harry Hosier must not be relegated to the past, but remembered and honored for the person that he was: a circuit rider who proclaimed the Good News of Jesus Christ. He represents the outreach of the church of his time. He is a symbol of his fellow laborers—his brother preachers—many unknown to us, but their names are recorded in the Lamb's Book of Life. Their ministry must be perpetuated. It is a legacy bequeathed to the contemporary preacher—the woman, the man—who today proclaims God's word.

SELECTED BIBLIOGRAPHY

Arminian Magazine for January 1794, The Experiences and Travels of Mr. Freeborn Garretson [sic], Minister of the Gospel, in North America. Extracted from the Narrative written by hi.self, and printed in Philadelphia in 1791.

Armstrong, James Edward. *History of the Old Baltimore Conference.* Baltimore: Printed for the Author, 1907.

Bangs, Nathan. *The Life of the Rev. Freeborn Garrettson.* New York: T. Mason and G. Lane, 1838.

Boehm, Henry. *Reminiscences, Historical and Bibliographical, of Sixty-Four Years in the Ministry.* New York: Carlton & Porter, 1865.

Colbert, William. *A Journal of the Travels of William Colbert Methodist Preacher Thro' Parts of Maryland, Pennsylvania, New York, Delaware and Virginia in 1790 to 1838.* Typescript Copy. Lake Junaluska, North Carolina: World Methodist Building.

Extracts of the Journals of the Rev. Dr. Coke's Five Visits to America. London: G. Paramore, 1793.

L. M. Hagood. *The Colored Man in the Methodist Episcopal Church.* 1890. Rpt. Westport, Conn.: Negro Universities Press, 1970.

Harrison, William P. *The Gospel Among the Slaves.* Nashville: Publishing House of the Methodist Episcopal Church, South, 1893.

Hurst, John Fletcher. *The History of Methodism.* New York: Eaton & Mains, 1902.

Journals and Letters of Francis Asbury. Ed. by Elmer T. Clark, J. Manning Potts, Jacob S. Payton. 3 vols. Nashville: Abingdon, Press, 1958.

Jones, Charles C. *The Religious Instruction of the Negroes in the United States.* 1842. Rpt. New York: Negro Universities Press, 1969.

Lednum, John. *A History of the Rise of Methodism in America.* Philadelphia: Printed for the Author, 1859.

Lee, Jesse. *A Short History of the Methodists in the United States of America.* Baltimore: Magill and Clime, 1810.

Licorish, Joshua E. *Harry Hosier, African Pioneer Preacher.* Philadelphia: Afro-Methodist Associates, 1967.

_____ "Harry Hosier." *Encyclopedia of World Methodism.* Ed. Nolan B. Harmon. 2 vols. Nashville: The United Methodist Publishing House, 1974.

Life Experiences and Gospel Labors of The Rt. Rev. Richard Allen . . . Written by Himself. Introduction by George A. Singleton. 1880. Rpt. New York: Abingdon Press, 1960.

"Minutes Taken at the Several Annual Conferences of the Methodist Episcopal Church for the Year 1788." In *Minutes of the Methodist Conference Annually Held in America; From 1773 to 1813, Inclusively.* New York: Daniel Hitt and Thomas Ward, 1819.

Negro History Bulletin. Vol. 3, no. 1.

Oates, John A. *The Story of Fayetteville and the Upper Cape Fear.* 2d ed. Raleigh, North Carolina: Litho Industries, Inc., 1972.

Raybold, G. A. *Reminiscences of Methodism in West Jersey.* New York: Lane and Scott, 1849.

Richardson, Harry V. *Dark Salvation.* Garden City, New York: Anchor-Press/Doubleday, 1976.

Seaman, Samuel A. *Annals of New York Methodism.* New York: Hunt & Eaton, 1892.

Smith, Warren Thomas. "The Incomparable 'Black Harry.' " *Together* 14:40-41.

_____ "Harry Hosier: Black Preacher Extraordinary." *The Journal of the Interdenominational Theological Center* 7:111-128.

Stevens, Abel. *History of the Methodist Episcopal Church.* 3 vols. New York: Carlton & Porter, 1864.

Washington, Booker T. *The Story of the Negro.* 2 vols. London: T. Fisher Unwin, 1909.